HAPPY CIRCLE
AND
FRIENDS

Written & Illustrated by

Dr. Geoffrey Phillips

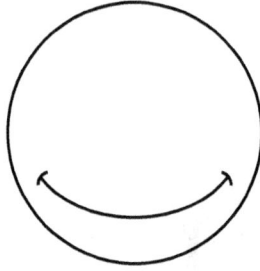

ABOUT THE AUTHOR

Geoffrey Phillips, M.D., resides in California and works as a physician. His practice over the years has included psychiatry, addiction medicine and cognitive therapy. He is board certified in both psychiatry and addiction medicine. He studied cognitive therapy at the Beck Institute in Philadelphia and is a member of the Academy of Cognitive Therapy. Prior to medicine, Dr. Phillips studied English and French Literature. He enjoys writing, creating books for all brains and all ages. He says he is rarely an Angry Cloud, sometimes an Anxious Egg and most often still a very Happy Circle.

ISBN 978-0-9893242-3-6

With love I dedicate these

Happy Circle Books

to my Happy Circles,

Breanna and Lauren.

HAPPY CIRCLE
MEETS
ANXIOUS EGG

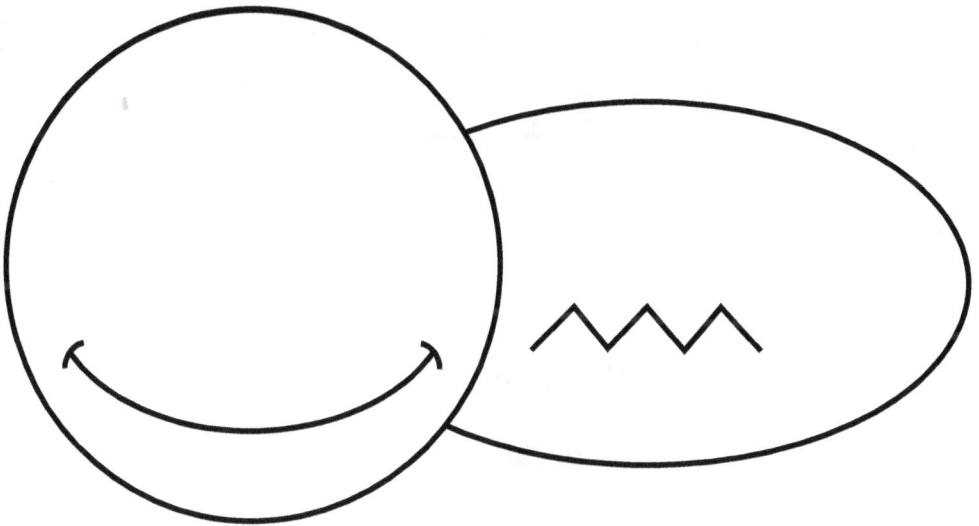

A Happy Circle

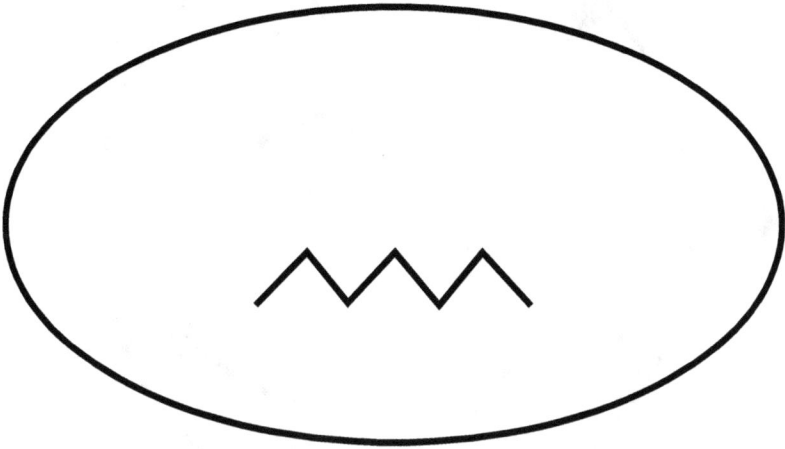

An Anxious Egg

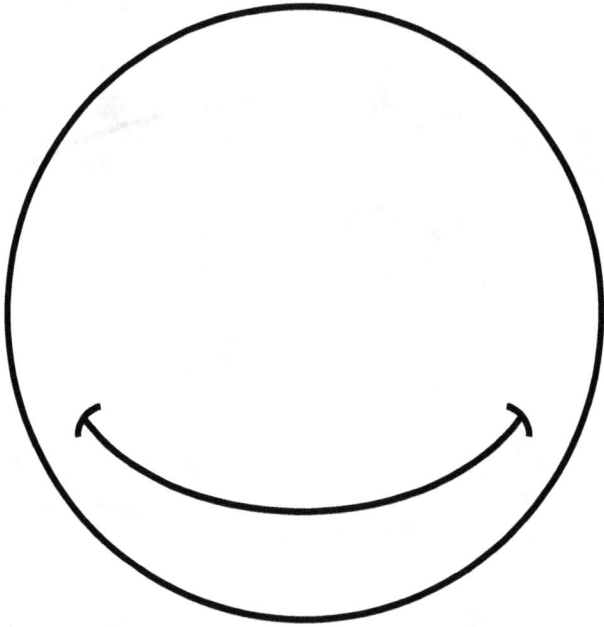

Still a very Happy Circle

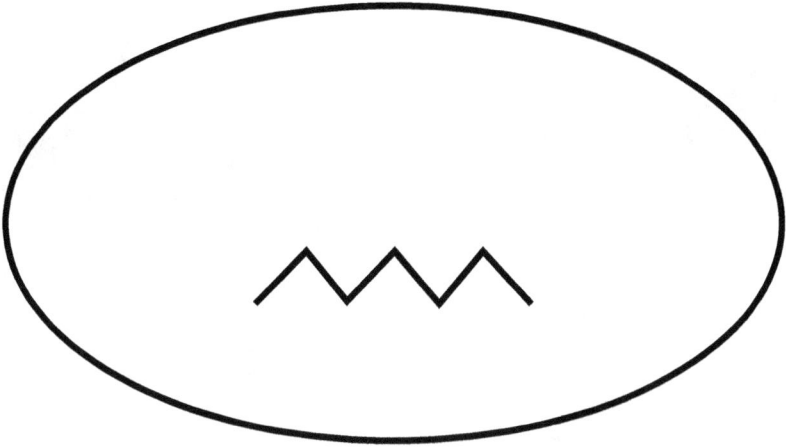

Still a worried, Anxious Egg

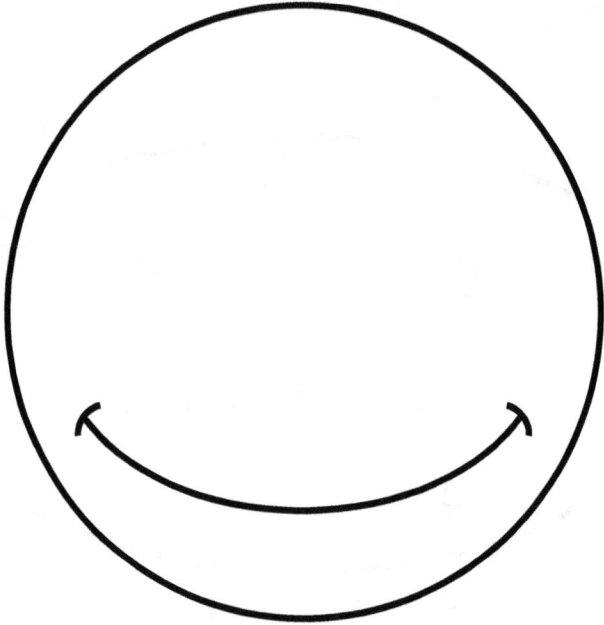

Happy Circle thinking what to say . . .

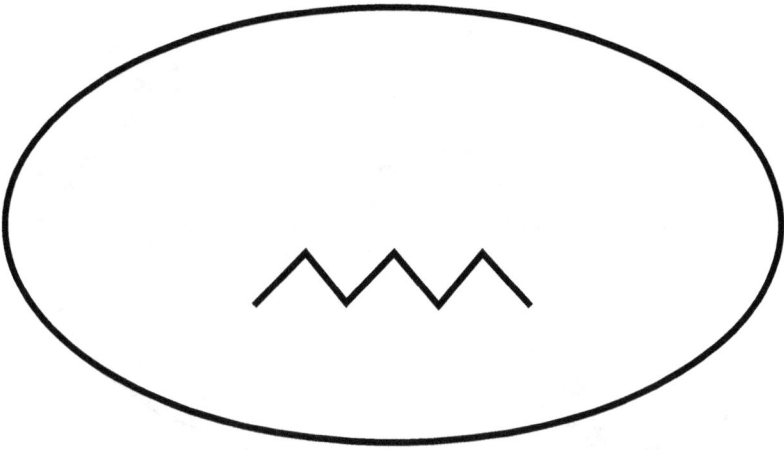

Anxious Egg saying what it thinks . . .

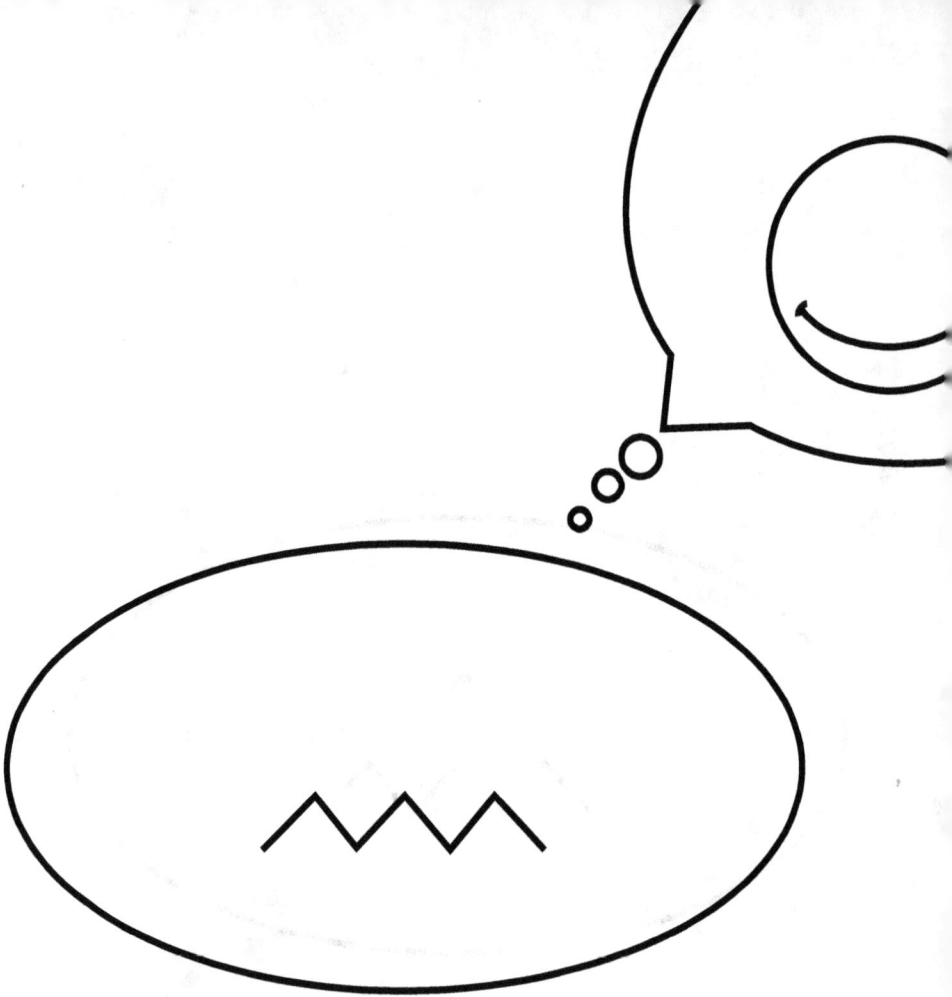

I used to be a Happy Circle, too . . .

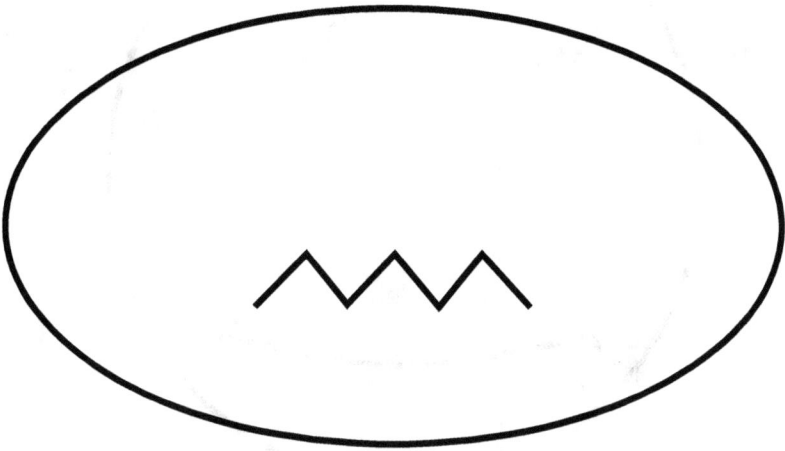

But then I changed into this worried,
Anxious Egg

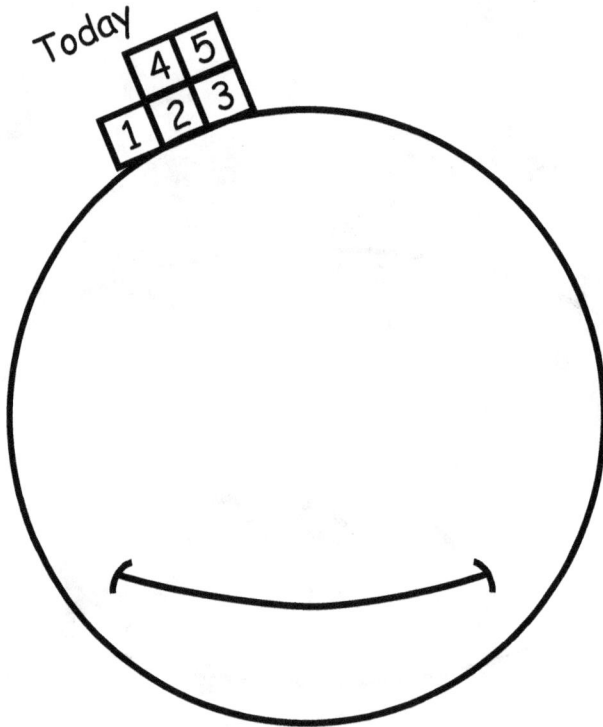

Today

4 5
1 2 3

I started to carry all the problems
of today, too much work, too much to do,
all the pressures, all the weight
on my poor head

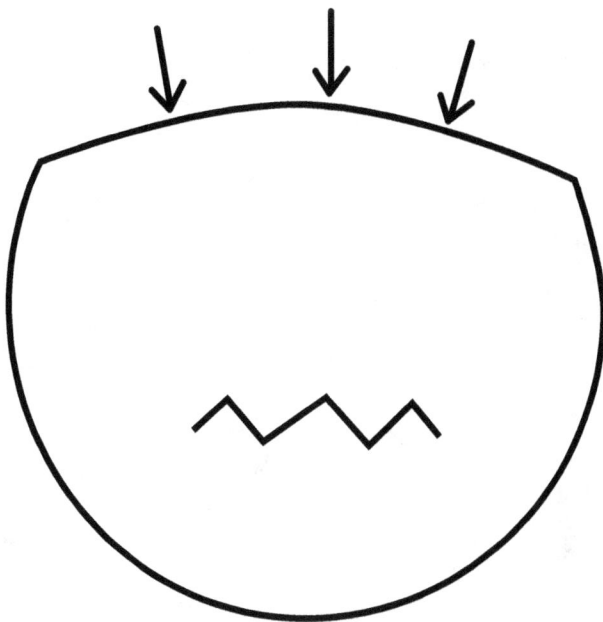

And I started to change shape

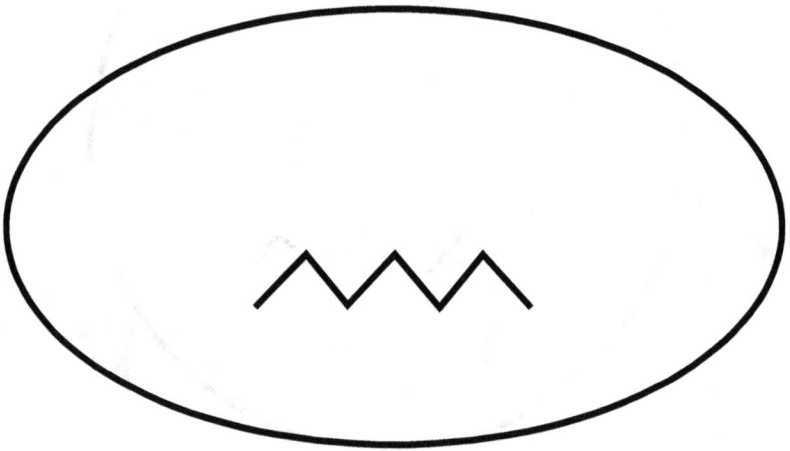

Then I worried about changing shape.
I was becoming an egg!

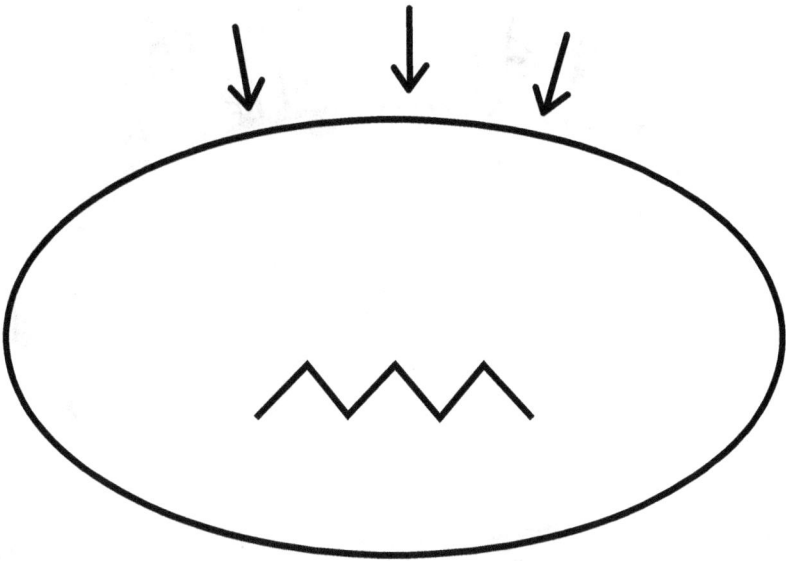

Worry worry worry
Pressure pressure pressure
Problems problems problems

Today

Tomorrow

4 5 6
1 2 3

4 5 6
1 2 3

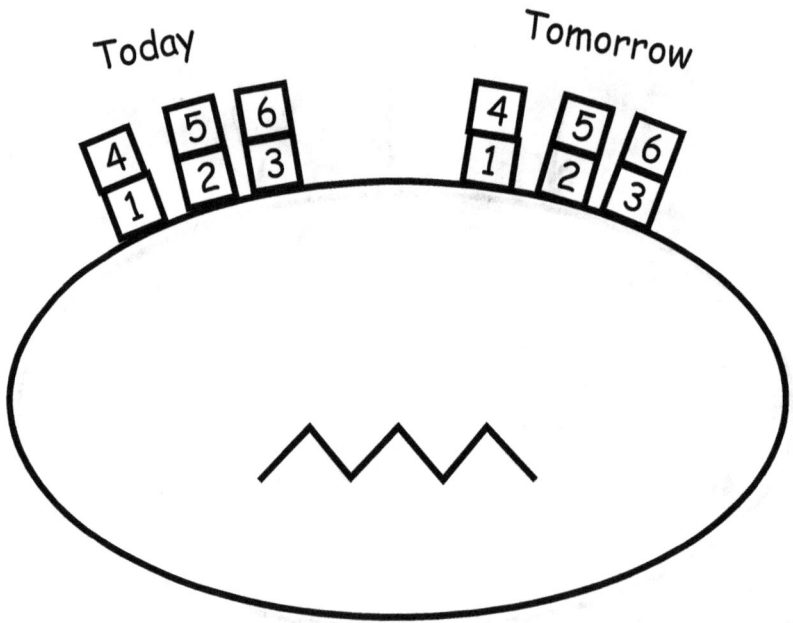

Soon I carried all the problems of
tomorrow, the future

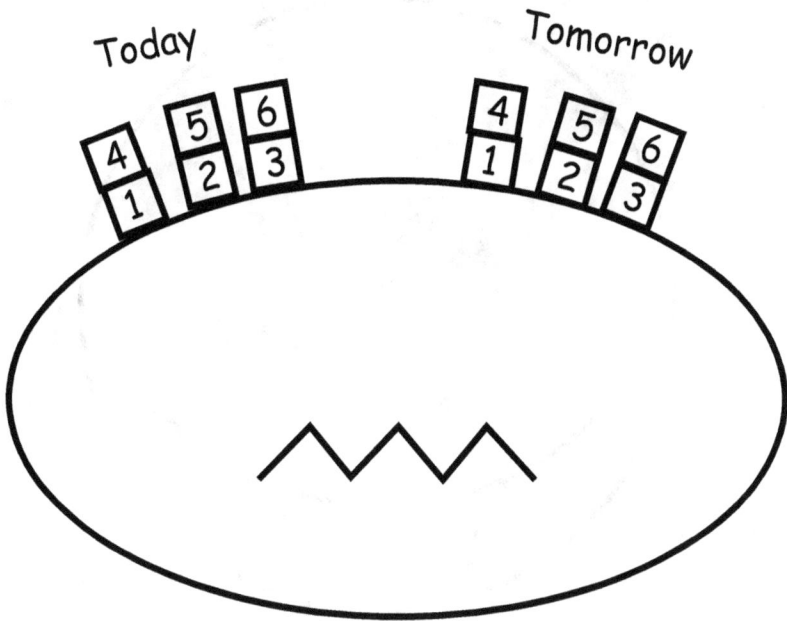

Today

Tomorrow

All the work I must do, all the challenges,
all the pressures and problems I will have,
all the weight that will be
put on my poor head

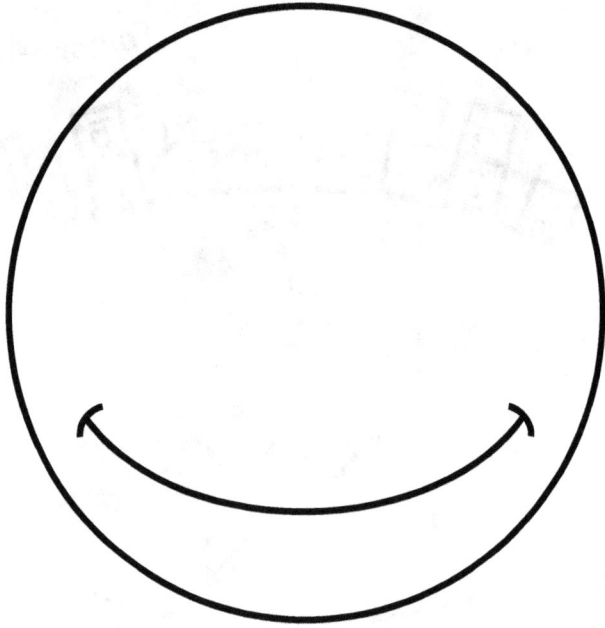

But I don't see anything on top
of your head, Anxious Egg

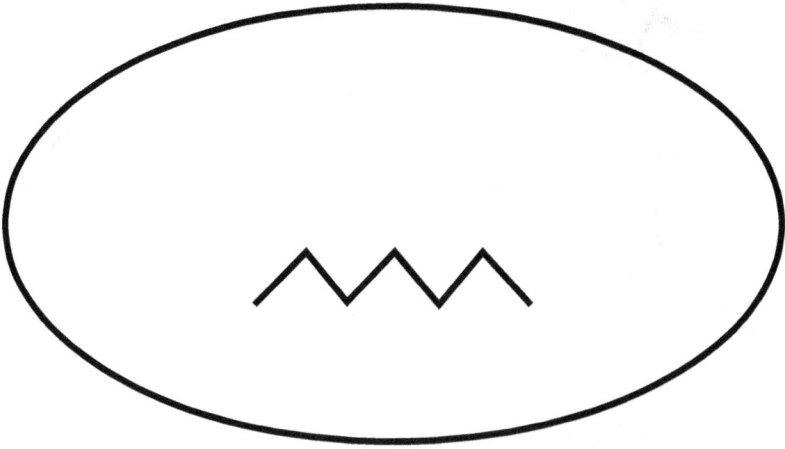

Oh, it's there alright, right on my head.
I feel it, Happy Circle.
You may not see it, but I feel it!

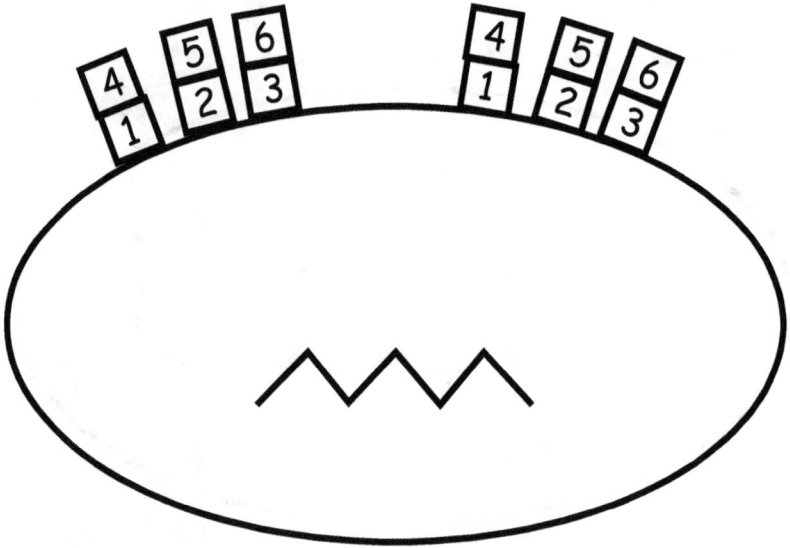

And now I worry my egg will crack!

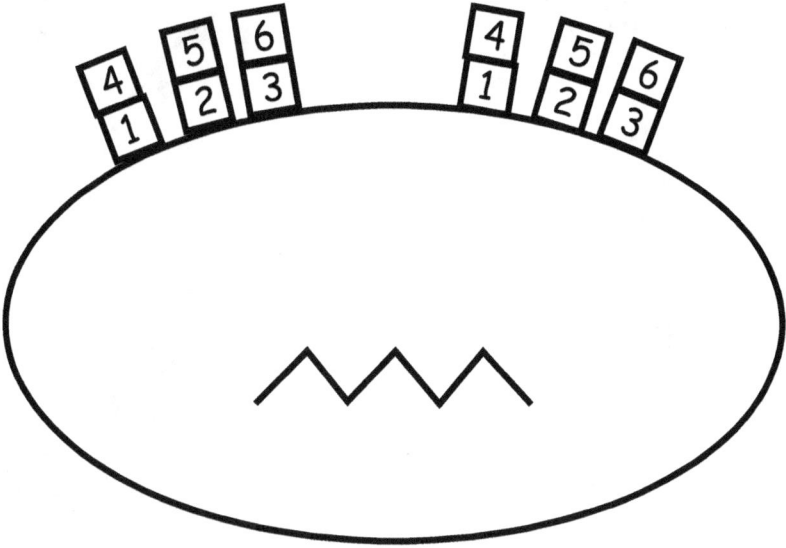

If my egg cracks under all this weight,
what will I do?

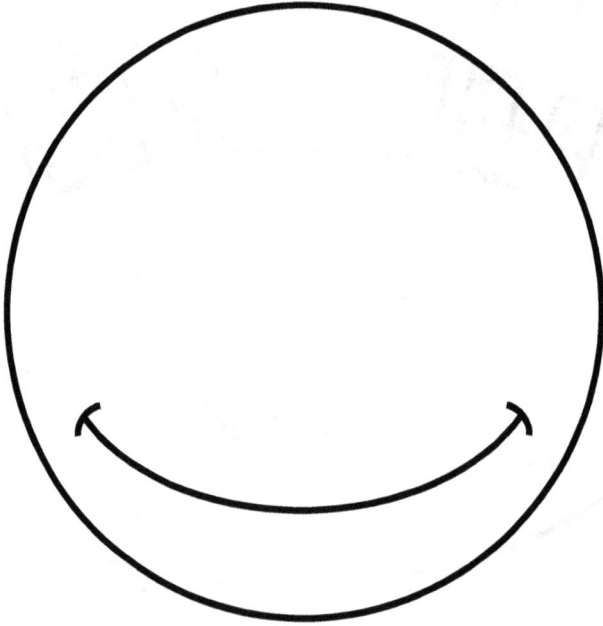

Can I help you, Anxious Egg?
Can I help you carry some of that?

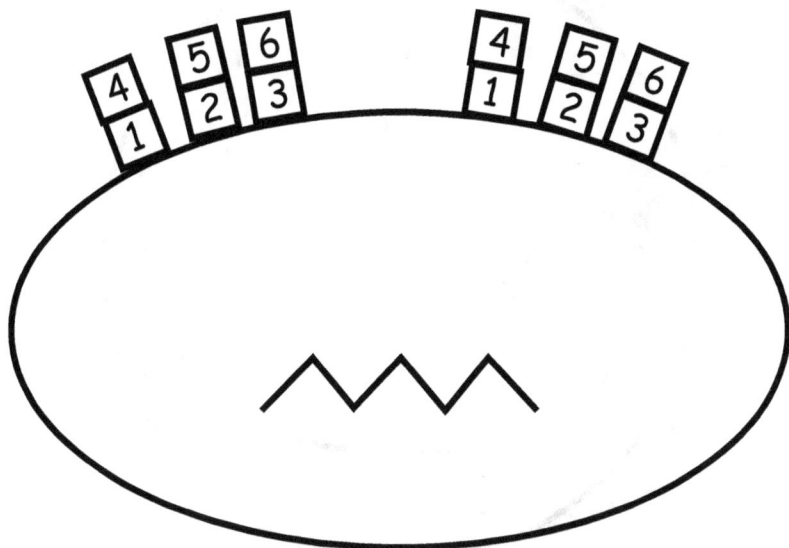

I don't know, Happy Circle.
I think it's too heavy.
I don't want you to be an egg like me.

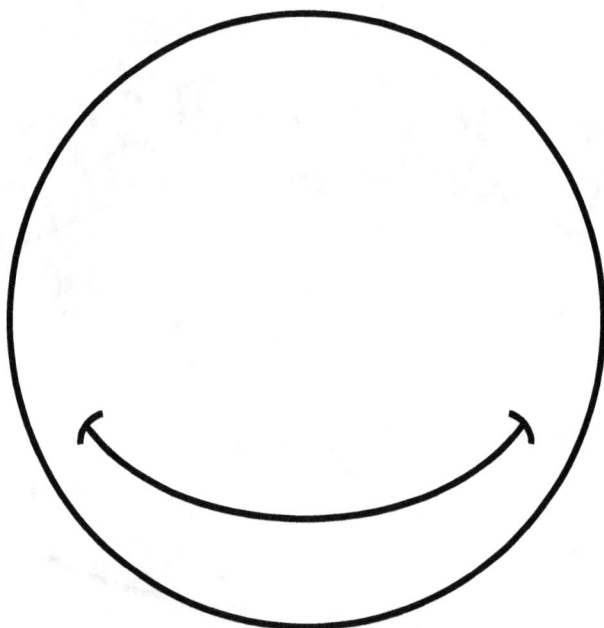

Maybe I can come next to you.
Maybe both of us can carry it?

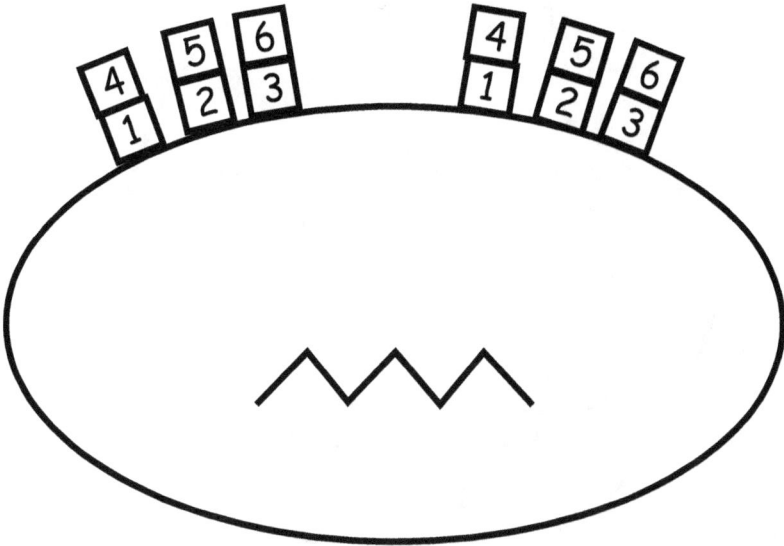

I don't know. Just let me crack.
You don't want to be an Anxious Egg
like that.

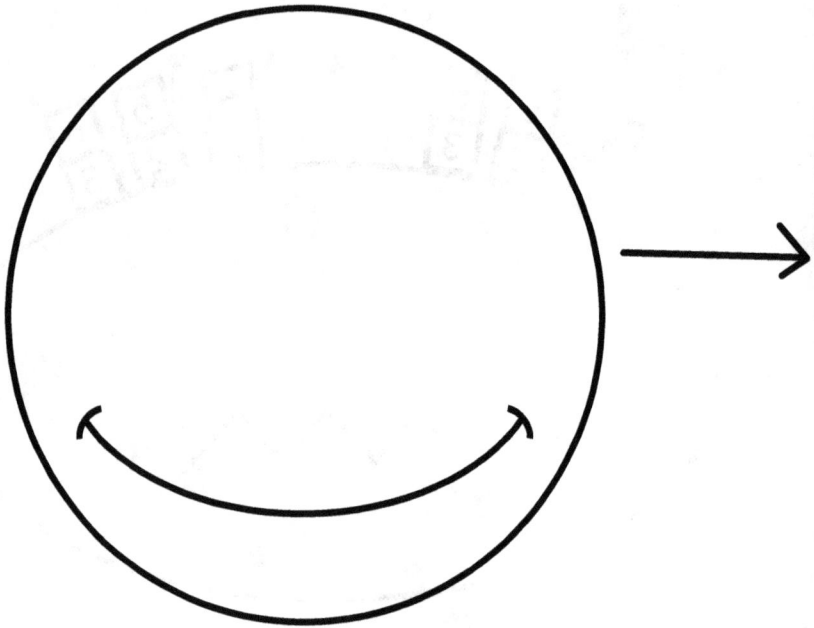

I will move next to you
and hold and carry my part

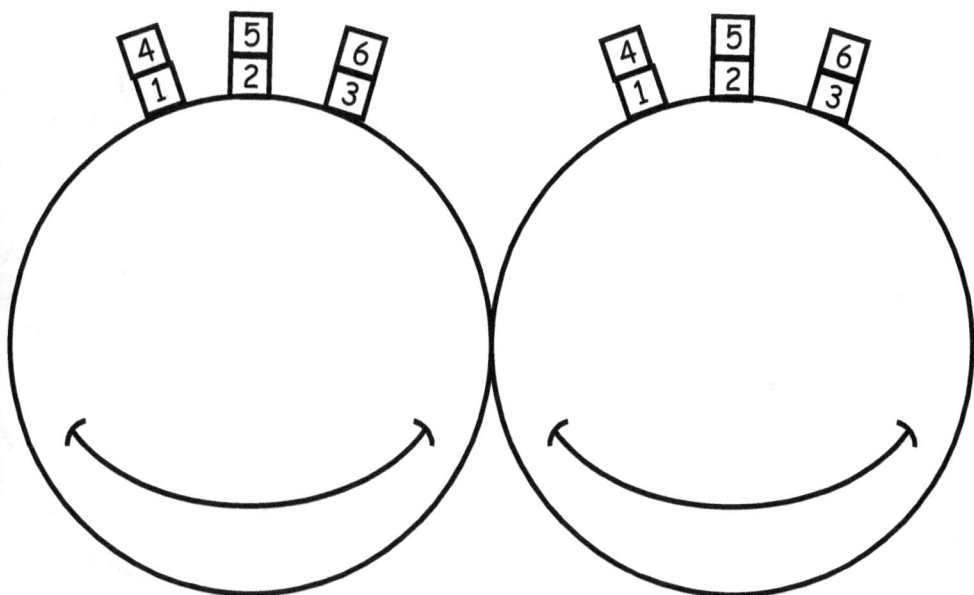

And we can be Happy Circles
together.

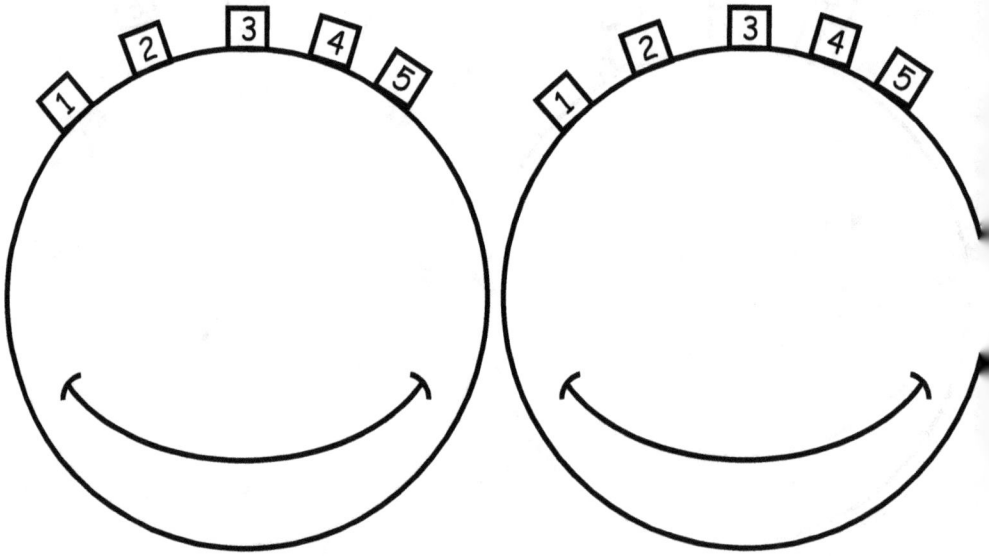

And if you have a lot of pressure,
a lot of worry,

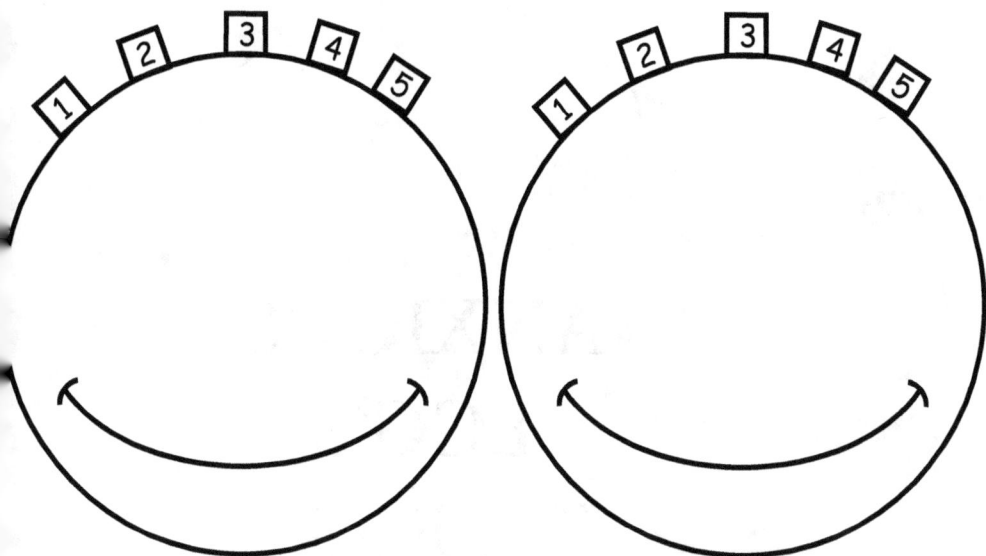

We may need four Happy Circles to help!

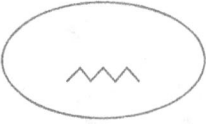

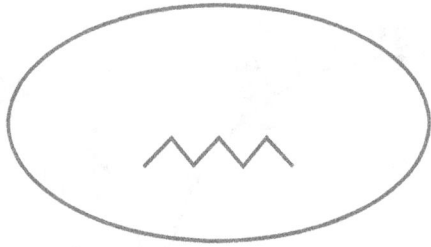

ANXIOUS
EGG'S
JOURNAL
PAGES

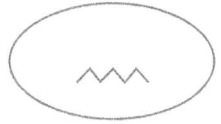

Use these next few pages to help you through times when you're feeling like an Anxious Egg. Answer the questions and write down your thoughts so that you can work your way back to being more like Happy Circle!

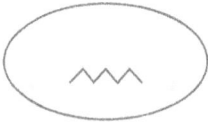

What makes your smile go squiggly like the Anxious Egg?

_____

_____

_____

_____

_____

_____

_____

_____

_____

How do you change into a worried, Anxious Egg?

_____

_____

_____

_____

_____

_____

_____

_____

_____

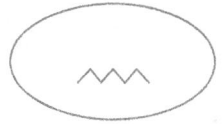

What are your problems of today?

_____

_____

_____

_____

_____

_____

_____

_____

_____

_____

"Pressure, pressure
pressure. Problems,
problems, problems."

What do you do when you feel so anxious?

_____

_____

_____

_____

_____

_____

_____

_____

_____

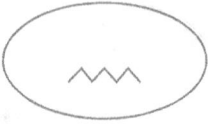

What are your problems of tomorrow?

_____

_____

_____

_____

_____

_____

"And now I fear my
egg will crack."

Who sees all those problems on your head?

_____

_____

_____

_____

_____

_____

_____

_____

_____

What resources do you bring to the problems?
(Education, intelligence, talent, time, money, hard work,
resolve, determination, strong will, persuasion, skills . . .)

_____

_____

_____

_____

_____

_____

_____

_____

_____

_____

Who's helping you? What else would help? Think
resources think support.

_____

_____

_____

_____

_____

_____

_____

HAPPY CIRCLE
MEETS
SAD TRIANGLE

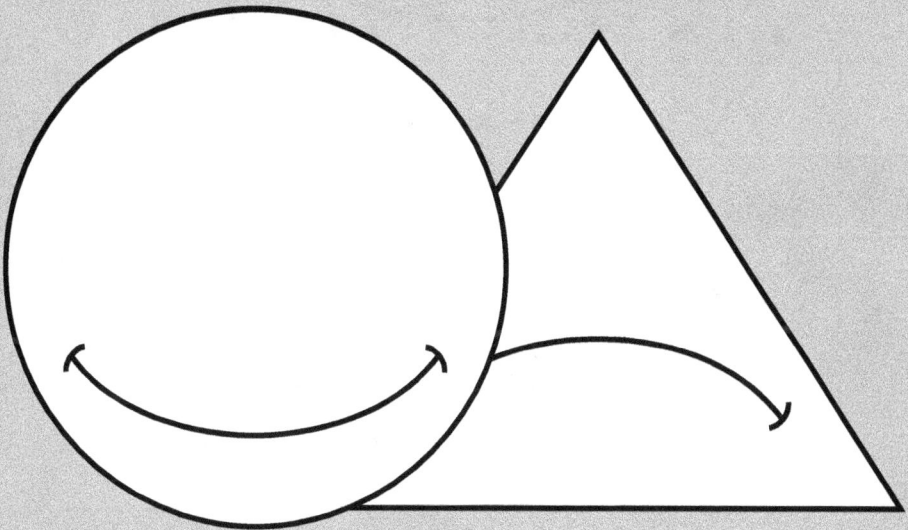

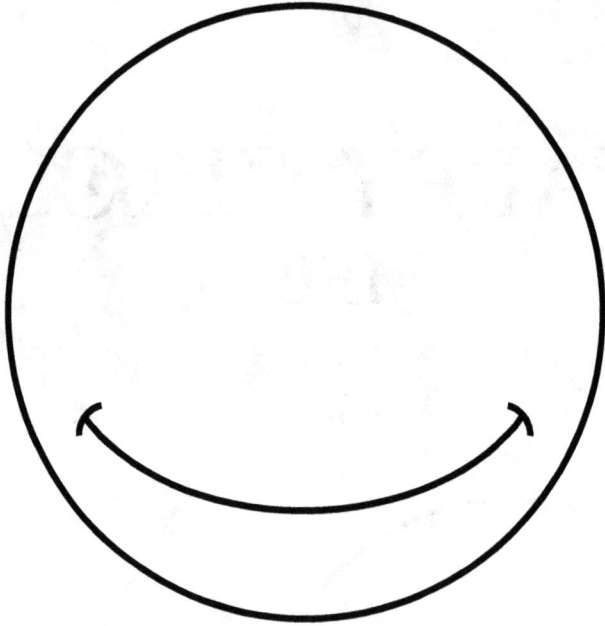

A Happy Circle

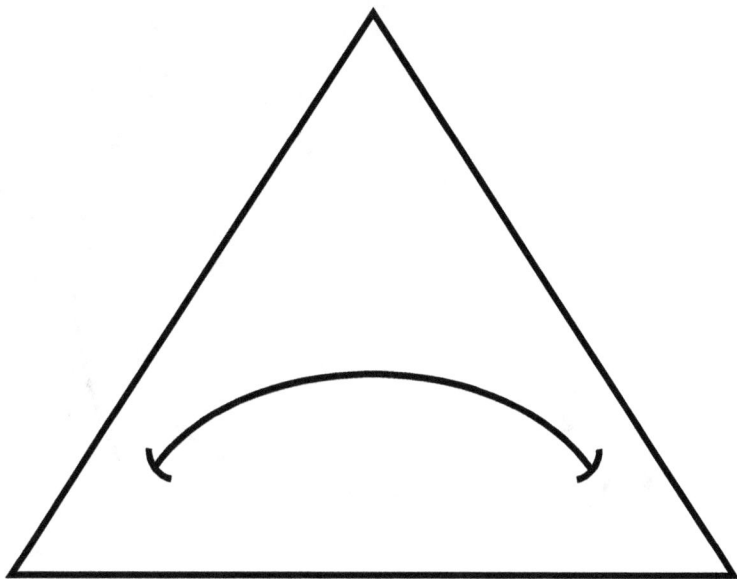

A Sad Triangle

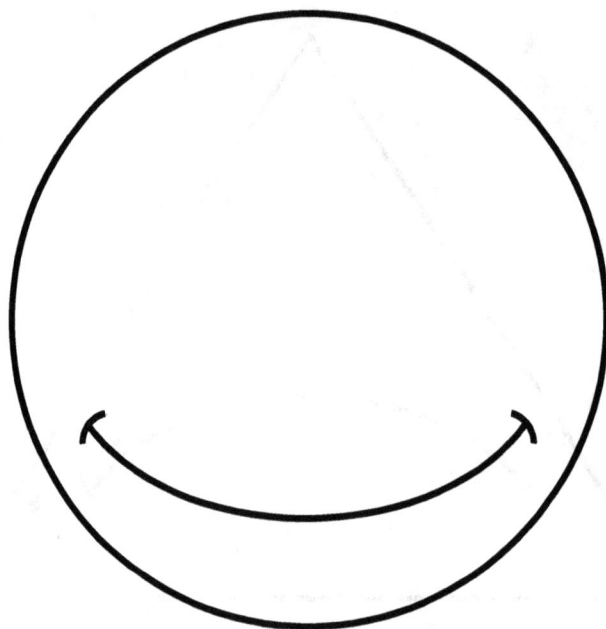

Still a very Happy Circle

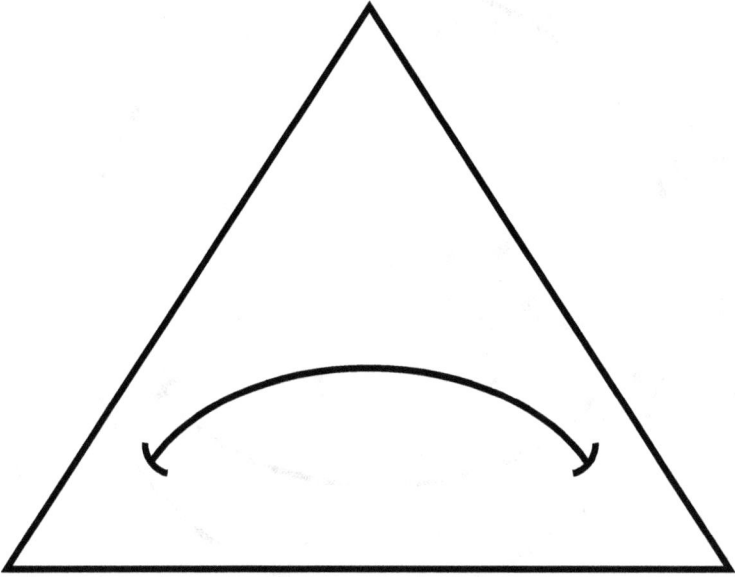

Still a depressed, Sad Triangle

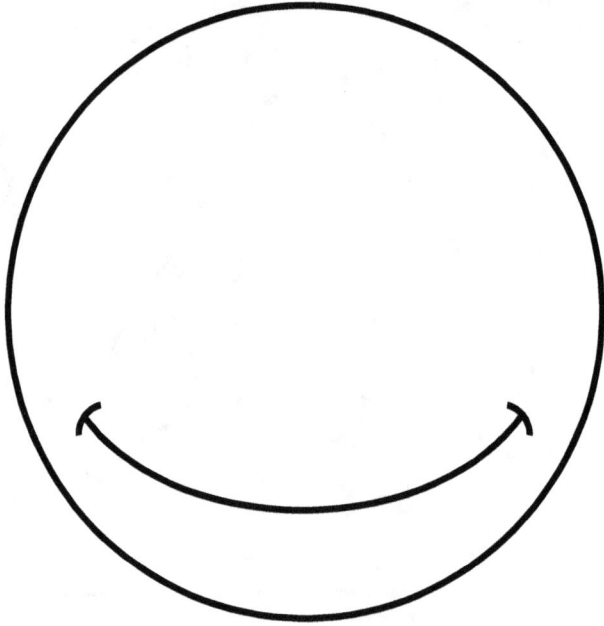

Happy Circle thinking what to say . . .

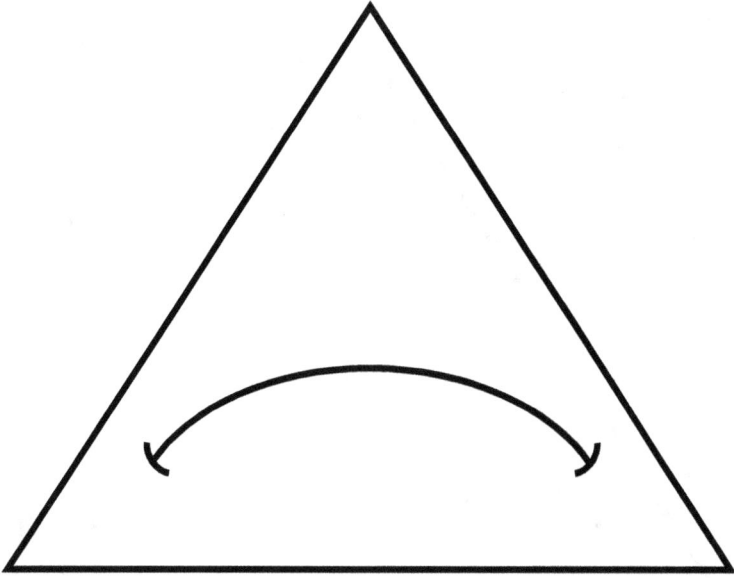

Sad Triangle saying what it thinks . . .

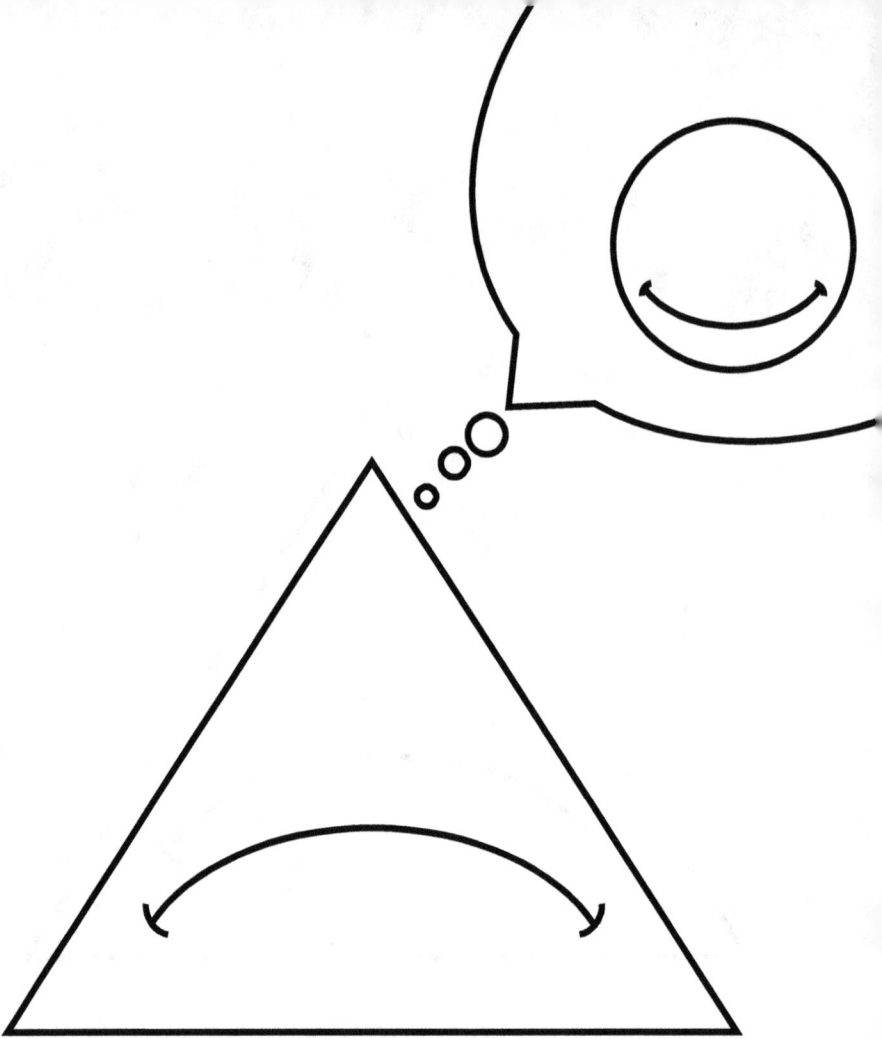

I used to be a Happy Circle, too

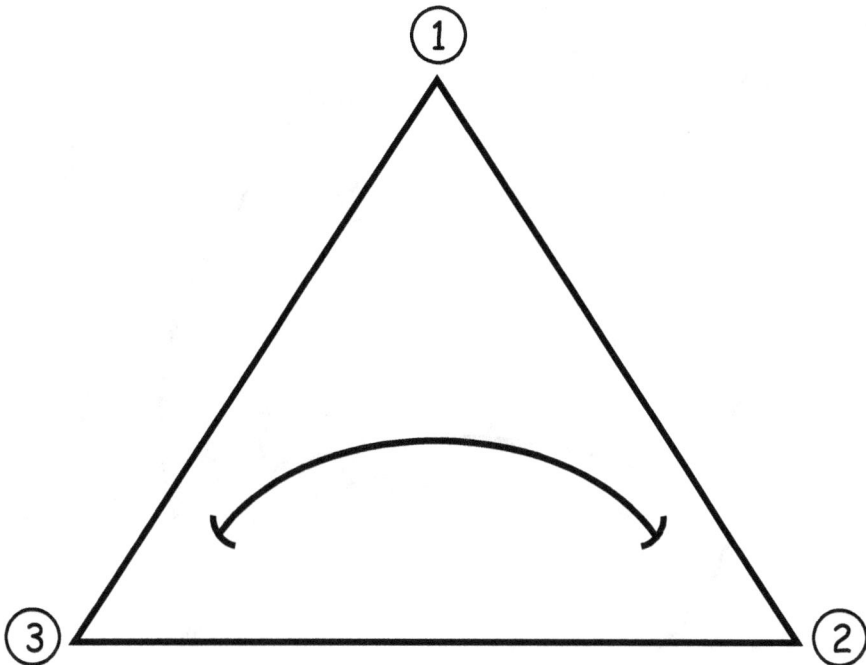

But then I started three Sad Angles
1 ... 2 ... 3 ...

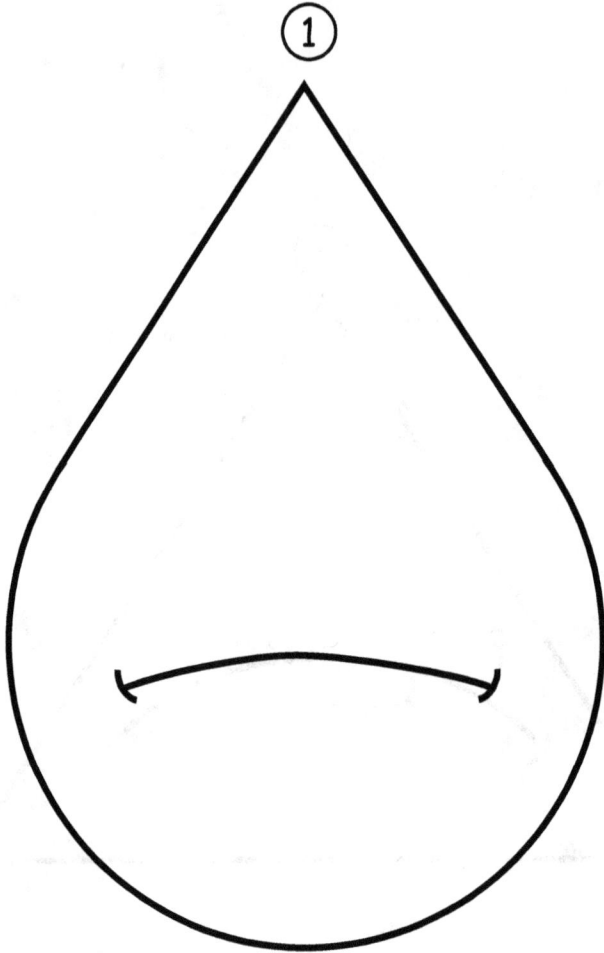

The first ① Sad Angle
was all about me!

I'm not good enough
I'm not smart enough
I'm too weak, not strong enough
I'm all alone
It's all my fault
I can't do anything right
I'm too slow, not fast enough
I'm just a burden
I'm   I'm   I'm
Me   me   me
Bad   bad   bad

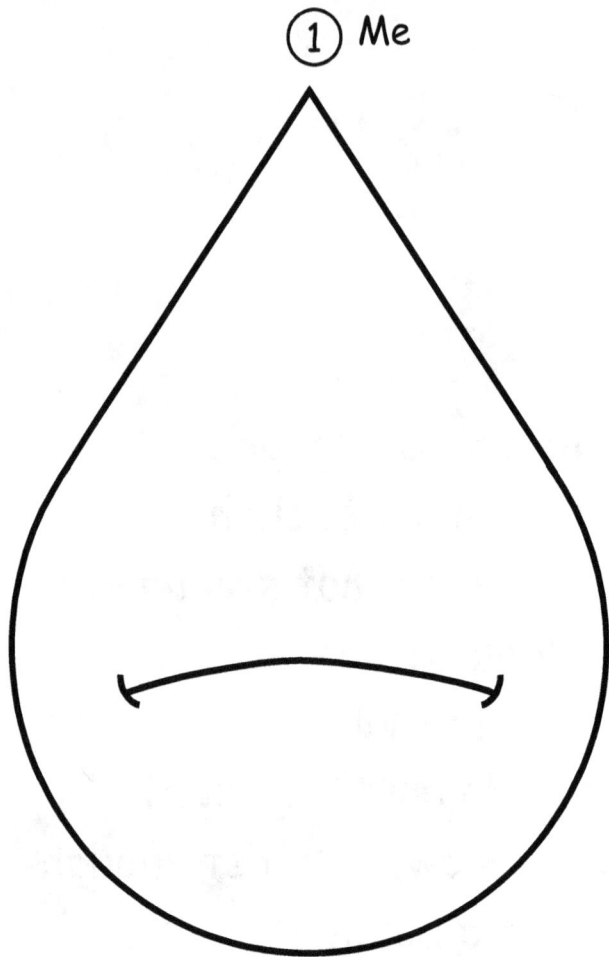

① Me

And I started to change shape

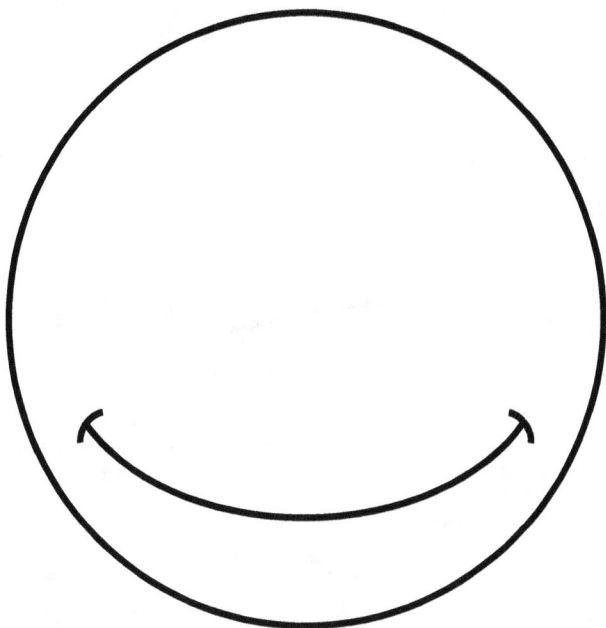

There are no angles in a Happy Circle

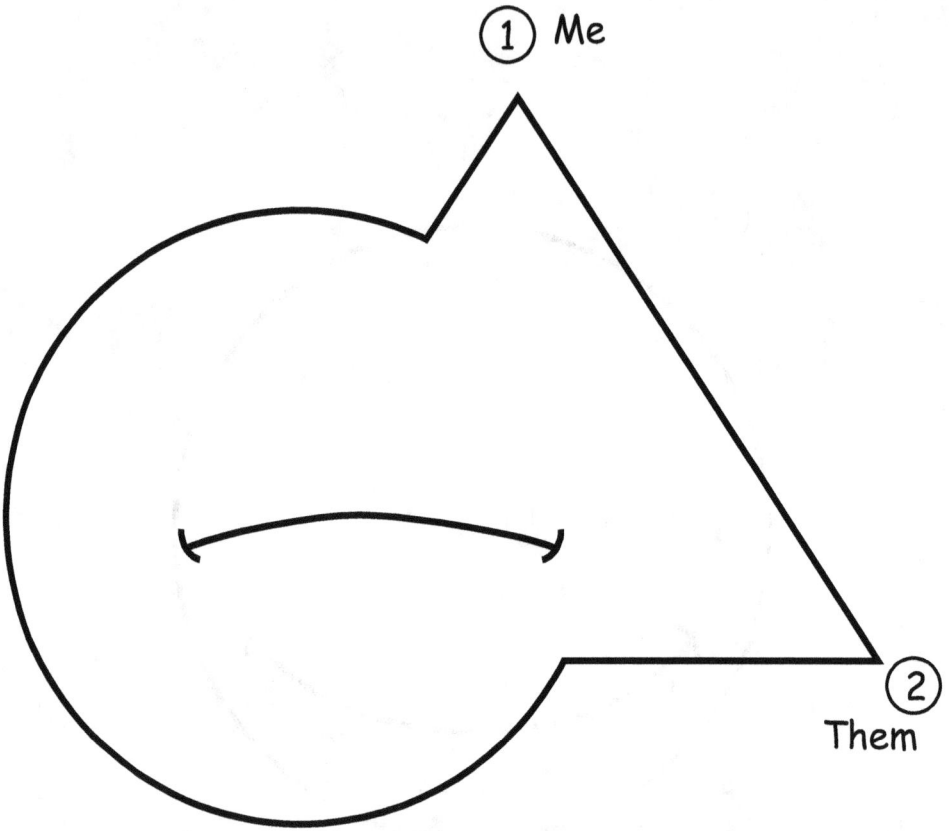

(1) Me

(2)
Them

The second ② Sad Angle
was all about them!

They don't like me
They don't want me
They don't think I'm good enough
They don't have a place for me
They don't think I'm strong
They think I'm all wrong
They think I'm weak
They just don't care, nobody cares
They don't even know I'm here
They   they   they
Them them them
Sad   sad   sad

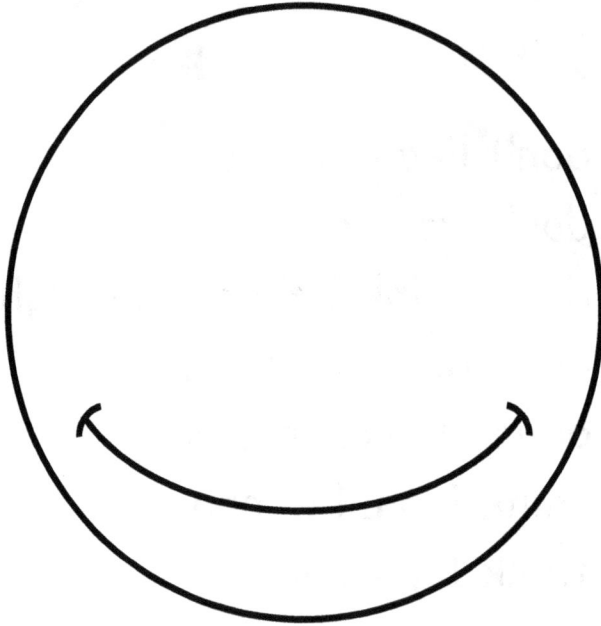

But what if I like you, Triangle?
Does that stop your second Sad Angle?
What if I do care?

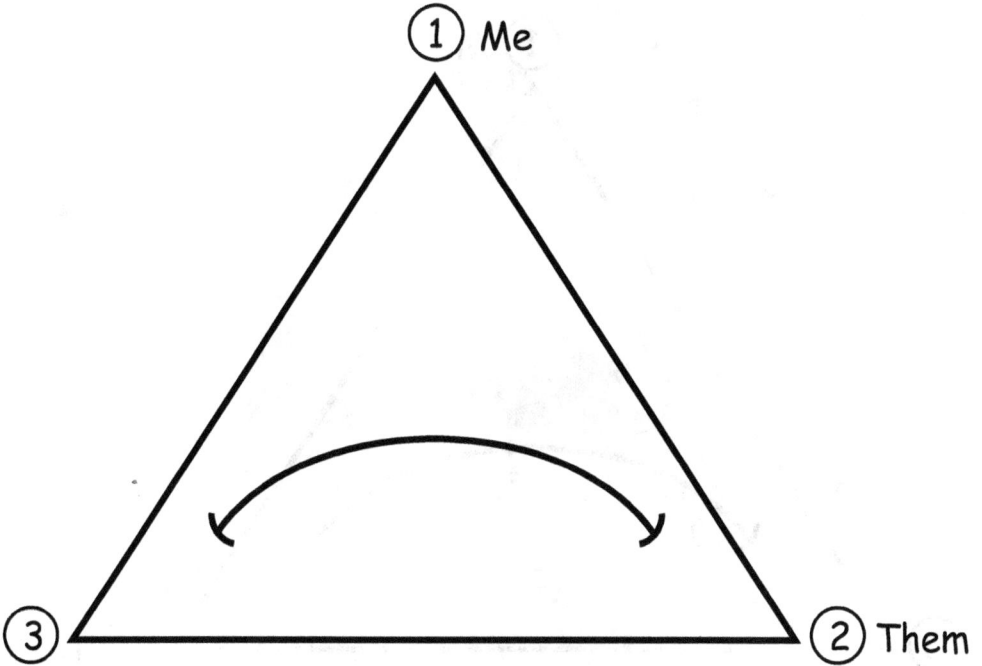

No, no, no Happy Circle.
My Sad Angle says
no you don't
and, no, you won't

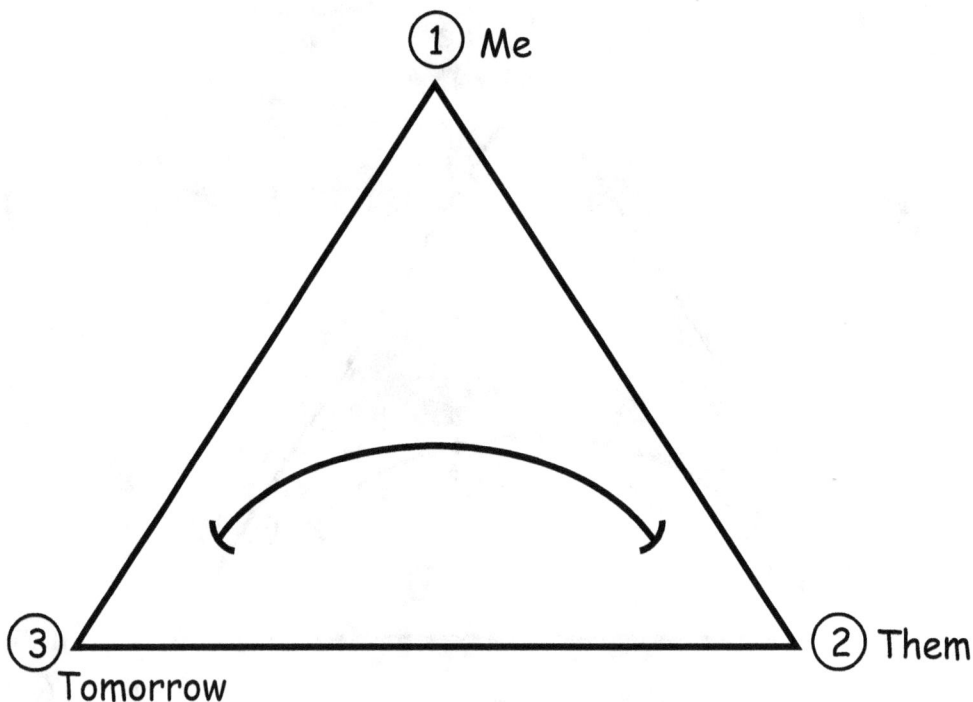

The third ③ Sad Angle
was all about tomorrow, the future.

This will never be good
This will never be right
I will always feel sad
It will stay this bad
I will stay this sad
I will always feel like this
I will always be a Sad Triangle
Will   will   will
Never never never

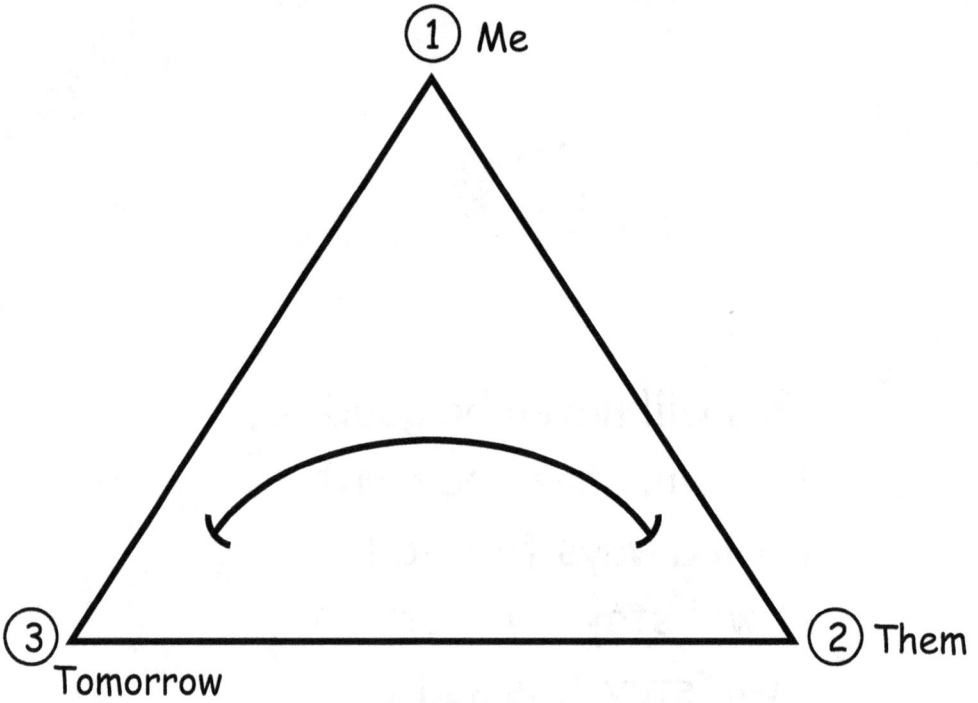

All my curves are gone

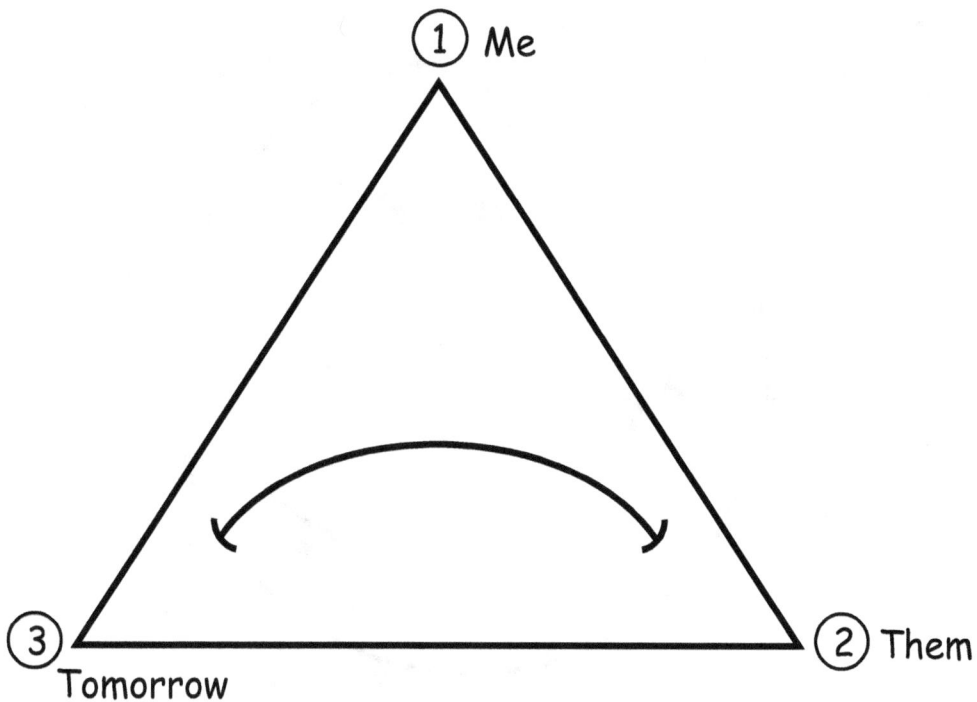

And I have only Sad Angles now . . .

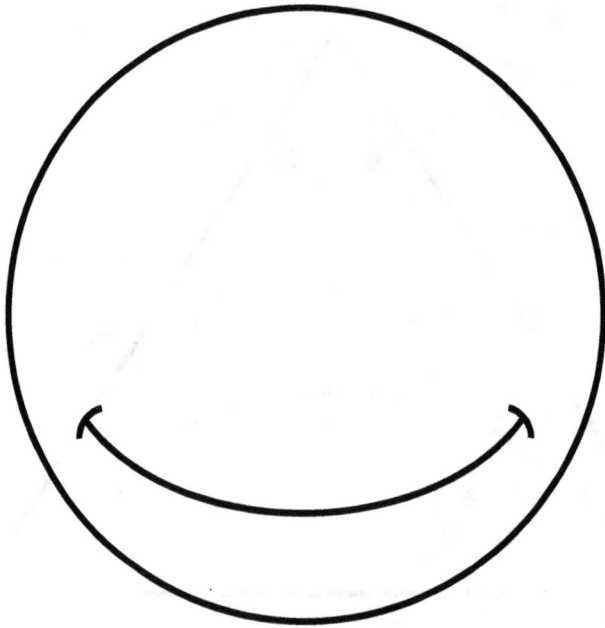

That's it, Triangle!
What if you think of only NOW,
only today?
Not tomorrow, not the future,
only today?

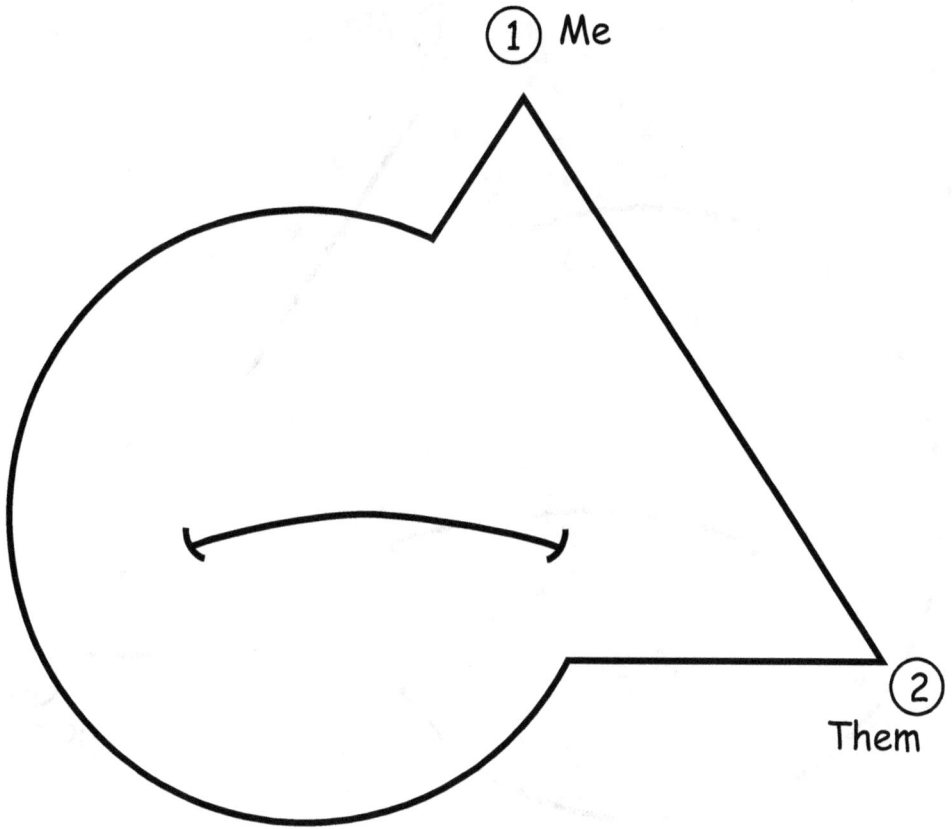

① Me

② Them

That stops one Sad Angle, right?

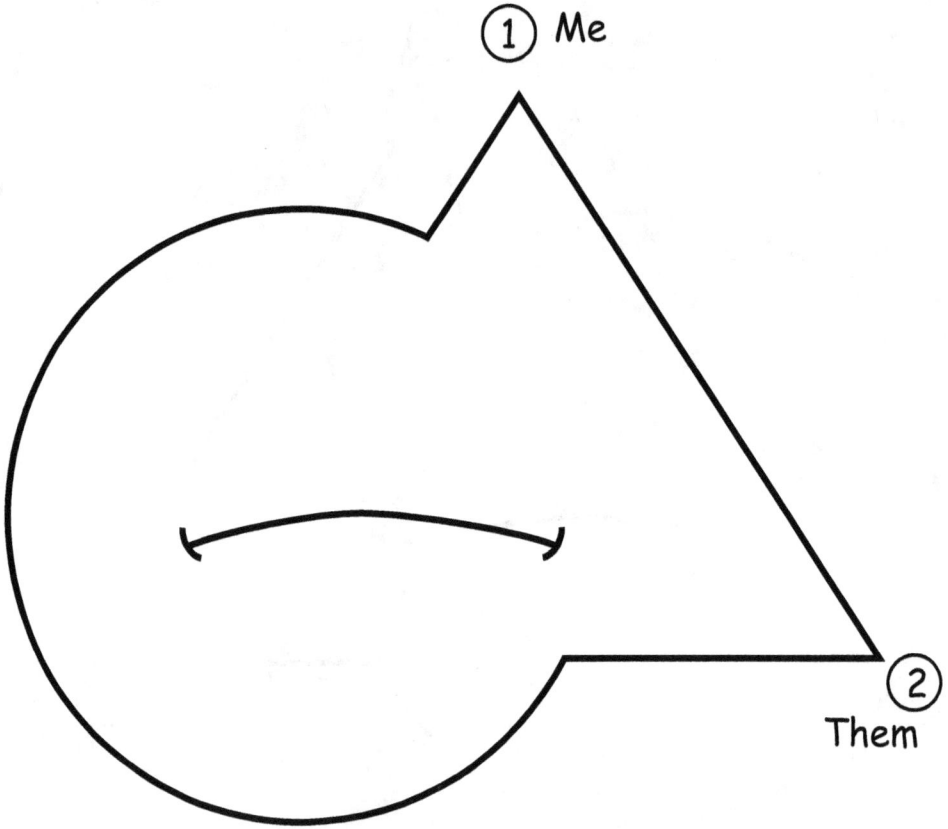

① Me

② Them

Maybe you're right, Happy Circle.
Let me try

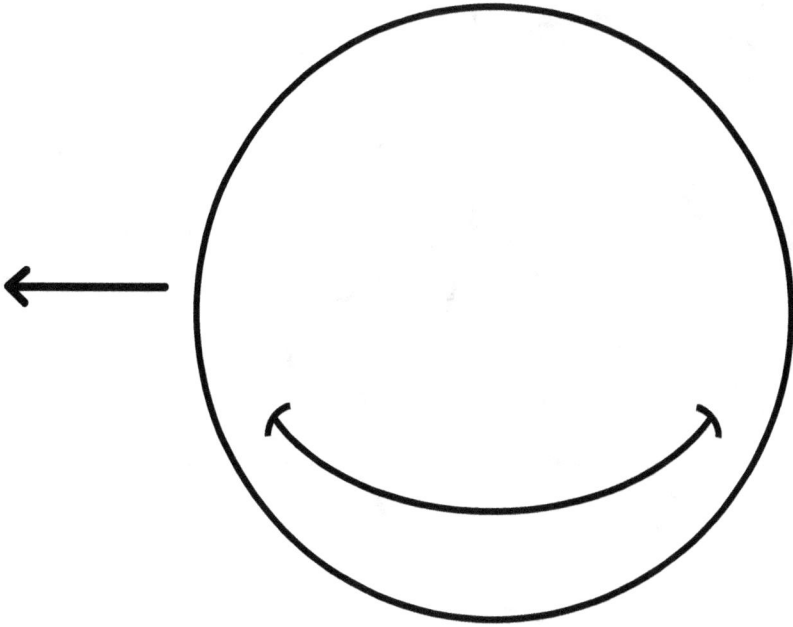

I don't know what to call
this new shape of yours,
but you're not a triangle anymore.

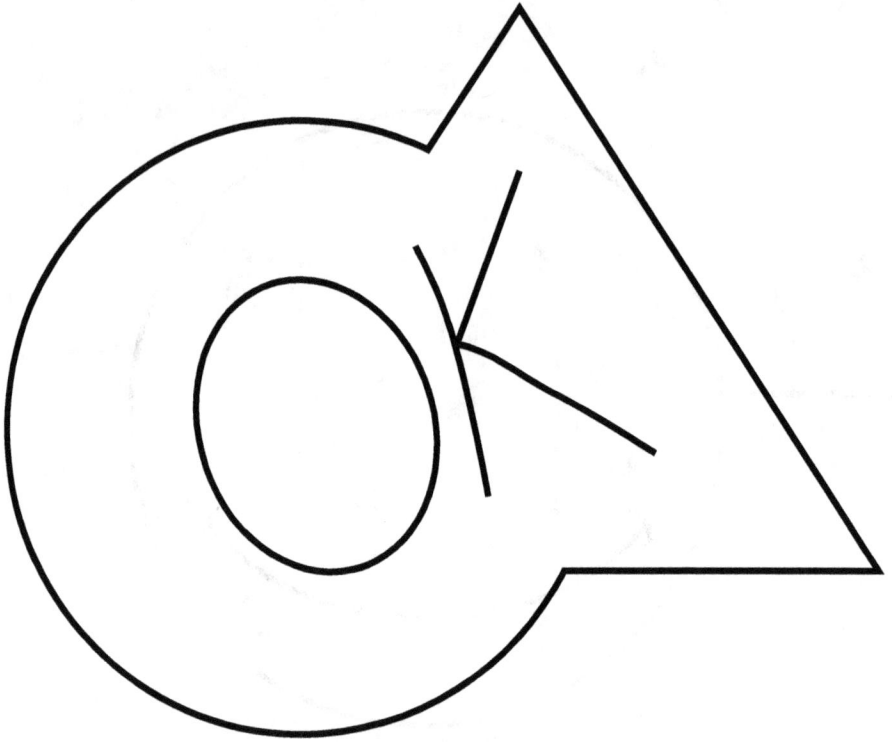

I think you are a "Circangle" now.
You look "OK"

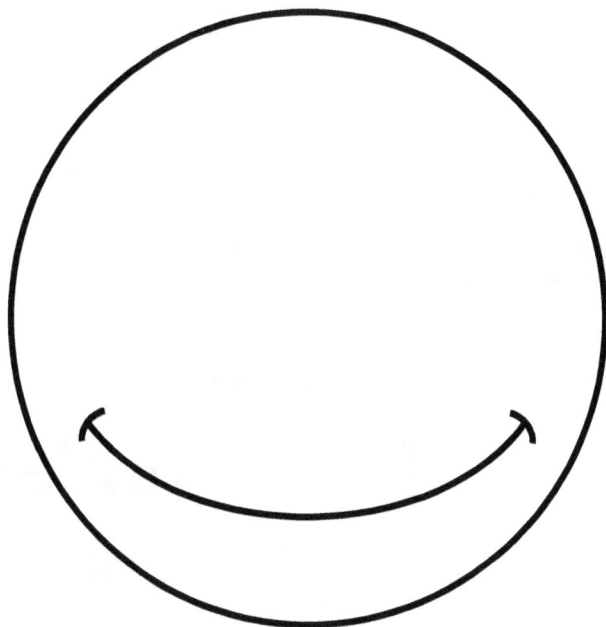

And soon will be a Happy Circle
again some day.

Two Sad Angles to go . . .

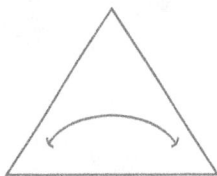

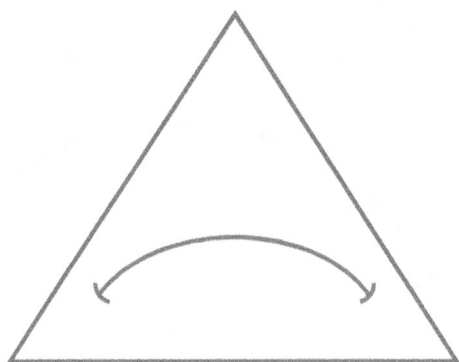

SAD
TRIANGLE'S
JOURNAL
PAGES

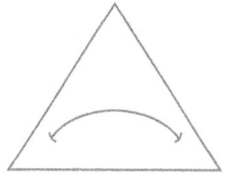

*Use these next few pages
to help you through times
when you're feeling like
a Sad Triangle.
Answer the questions and
write down your thoughts
so that you can work
your way back to being
more like Happy Circle!*

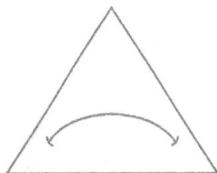

The First Sad Angle was all about me!
Why the Sad Angle?

_____

_____

_____

_____

_____

_____

_____

_____

You feel most sad when you think about what?

_____

_____

_____

_____

_____

_____

_____

_____

_____

_____

_____

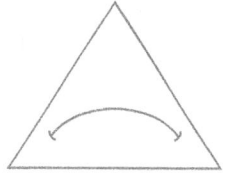

Two (2) Sad Angles ("Circangle"): Which Sad Angles are they? Me me me? Them them them?

_____

_____

_____

_____

Write about the times you have had Two Sad Angles. What is happening at those times? What are the situations?

_____

_____

_____

_____

_____

_____

_____

Can you draw your own "Circangle"?

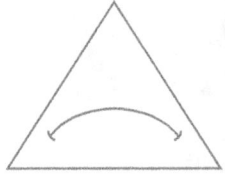

Three Sad Angles. What are your thoughts? Try to put them into three angles.

_____
_____
_____
_____
_____
_____
_____
_____

"All my curves are gone."

Why does Happy Circle tell "Circangle", "You look 'OK'"?

_____
_____
_____
_____
_____
_____
_____
_____

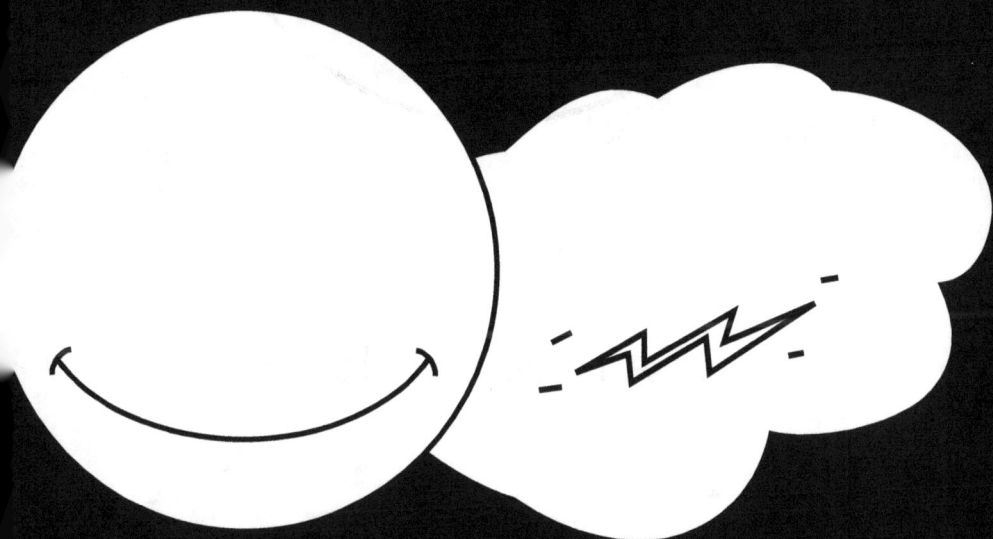

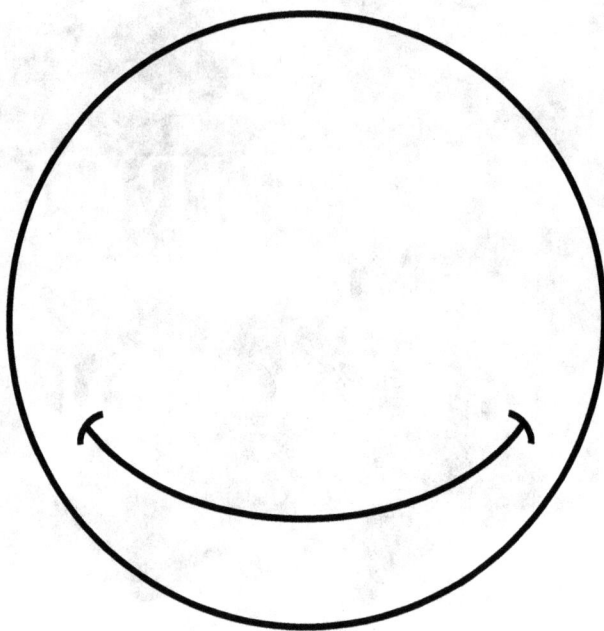

A Happy Circle

An Angry Cloud

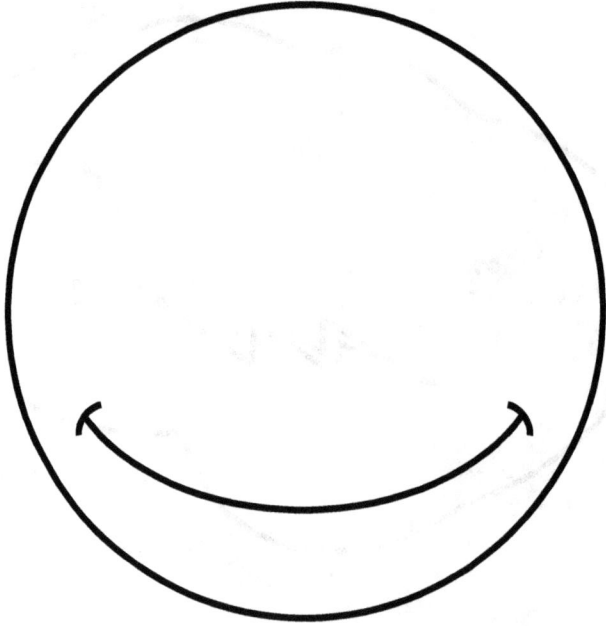

Still a very Happy Circle

Still a very Angry Cloud

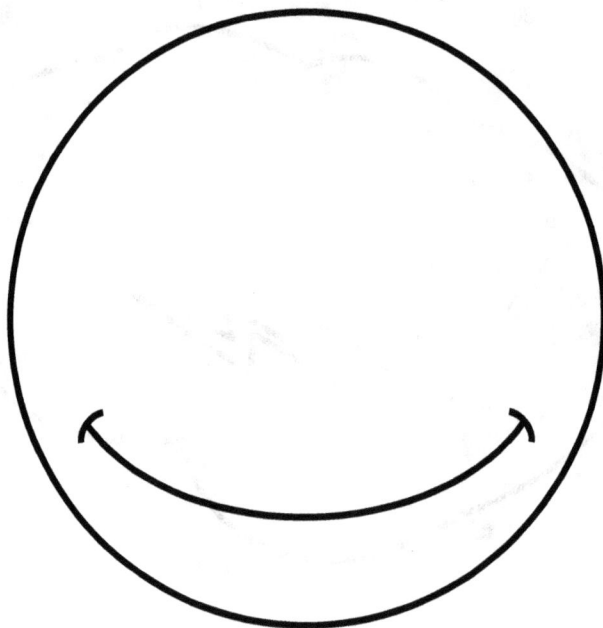

Happy Circle thinking what to say . . .

Angry Cloud saying what it thinks . . .

I used to be a Happy Circle, too . . .

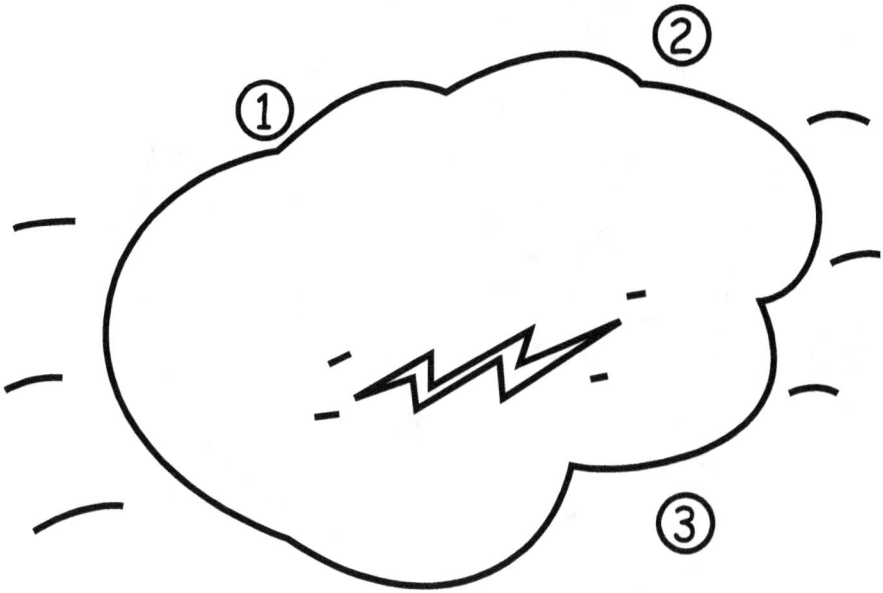

But then I started three Angry Clouds
1 . . . 2 . . . 3 . . .

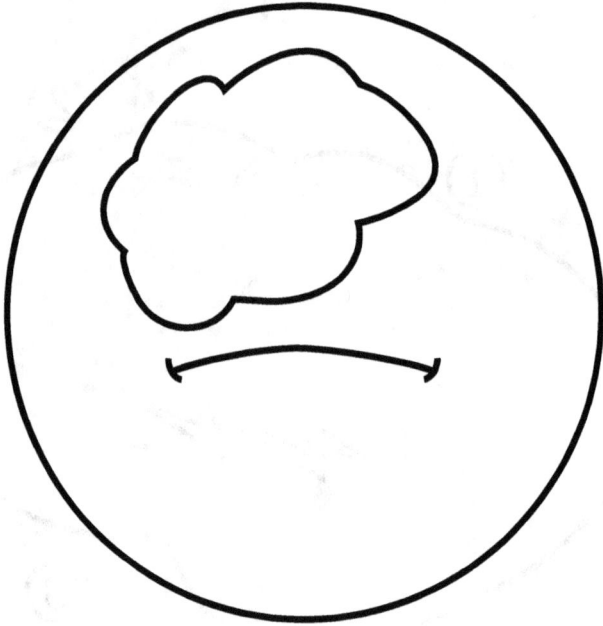

The clouds covered
my Happy Circle

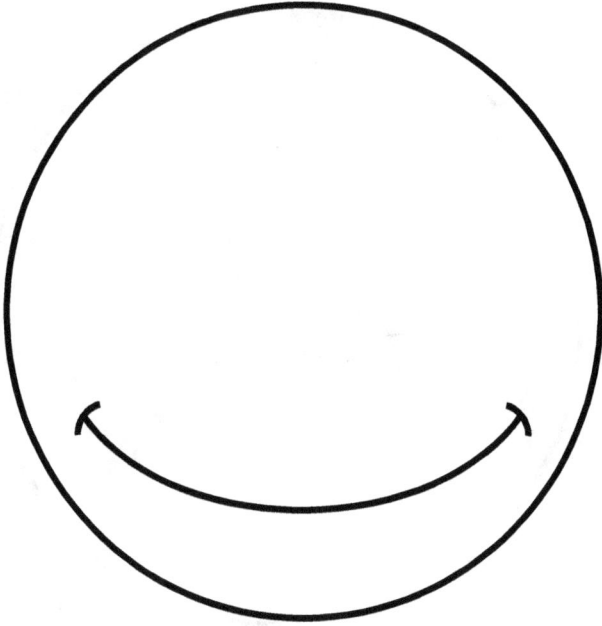

There are no storm clouds
on a Happy Circle

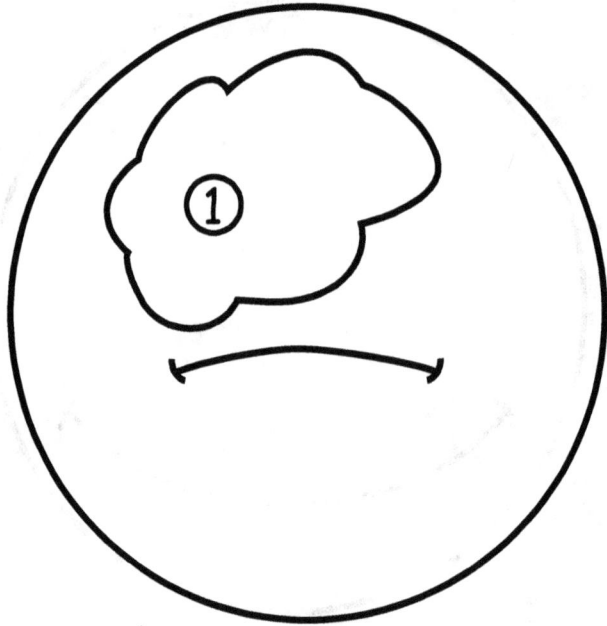

The first ① Angry Cloud
was all about fairness to me!

That's not fair
You cut in front of me
He took it from me
I deserve just as much, or more
You listened to her, not to me
He got more than I
Why should I, when they don't?!
I was here first
That was mine, not yours
If she gets one, I should get one
I   I   I
Me   Me   Me
Not fair not fair

Soon I changed shape

And my head was full of booming thunder
and bolts of lightning!

The second ② Angry Cloud
was all about justice and
what's right!

That's not right to blame
It's not right to have so much work
It's not right for parents to fight
It's not right to make fun of people
It's not right to spank children
People don't obey their own rules —
  it's just not right!
It's not right to have so much pain
God is not helping yet —
  it's just not right
Not right not right
It's just not right

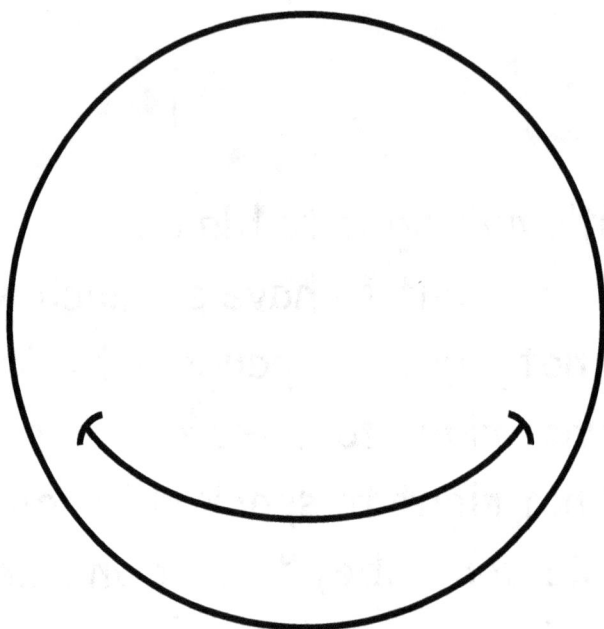

But is it right to make these storms?
Can I help you clear the clouds away?

No, stay away, Happy Circle.
My lightning will strike,
and my thunder will boom!

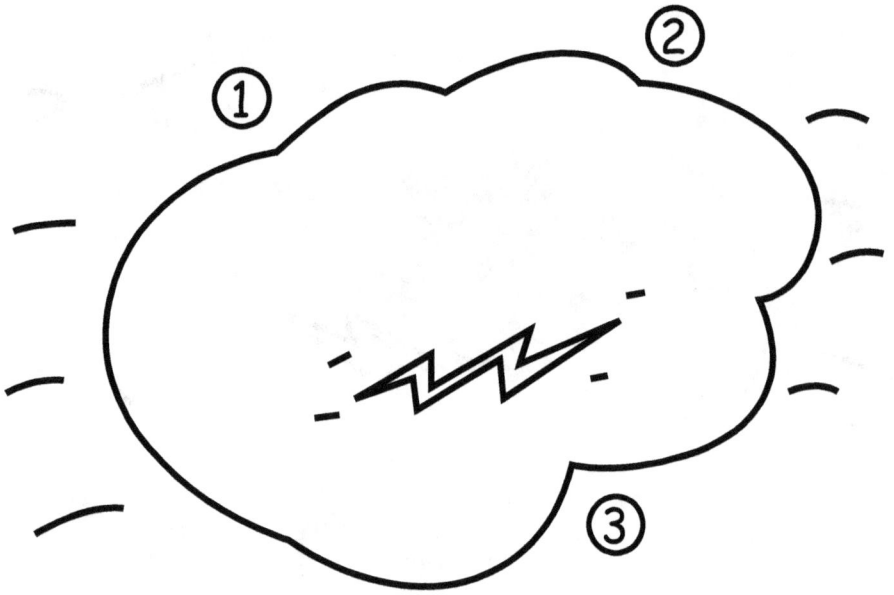

The third ③ Angry Cloud
was all about hurt!

It hurts me when you say that
Don't call me names
You insulted me
You went behind my back
You were mean to me
Stop making fun of me
Stop mistreating me
You broke our promise
I thought you were my friend
Hurt hurt hurt
Pain pain pain

Now the Angry Clouds are dark and loud.
I can hardly think.
I can hardly see.

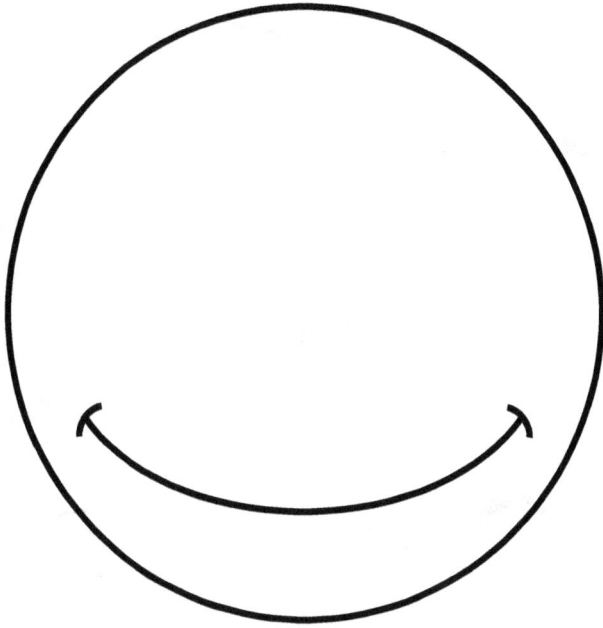

I don't see the lightning, Angry Cloud.
I don't hear any booms.

Don't you see, Happy Circle,
I'm holding it in?!

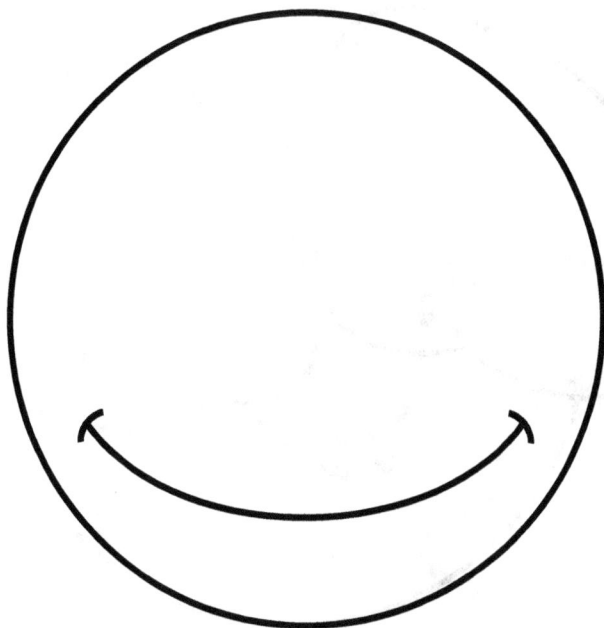

That's it, Angry Cloud!
What if you let go?
Let go of the clouds.
And we can talk, talk, talk
until the clouds go away . . .

Maybe you're right, Happy Circle.
I can give it a try

I will see clearly
without these clouds in my eye.

Two Angry Clouds to go . . .

ANGRY CLOUD'S JOURNAL PAGES

Use these next few pages to help you through times when you're feeling like an Angry Cloud. Answer the questions and write down your thoughts so that you can work your way back to being more like Happy Circle!

"All about fairness to me!" What hasn't been fair to you? List everything.

_____

_____

_____

_____

_____

_____

_____

_____

_____

_____

_____

_____

_____

_____

_____

_____

_____

What hasn't been right? What is the injustice? Write it out and think it out. Put it into words and put it on paper.

_____

_____

_____

_____

_____

_____

_____

_____

_____

_____

_____

_____

"Not right, not right; it's just not right."

_____

_____

I feel hurt or mistreated . . . so mad "I can hardly think. I can hardly see." A three (3) cloud moment can happen when something seems unfair to me, it would be wrong and unjust if it happened to anyone, and it hurts emotionally! All three clouds at once! Can you describe your own Three Cloud Moment?

_____

_____

_____

_____

_____

_____

_____

_____

_____

_____

_____

_____

_____

_____

_____

_____

_____

_____

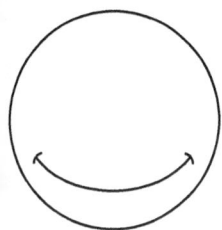

Happy Circle Resources

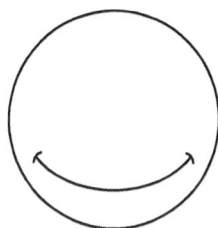

ORGANIZATIONS/WEBSITES:

Association for Behavioral and Cognitive Therapies

www.abct.org

Academy of Cognitive Therapy

www.academyofct.org

Beck Institute for Cognitive Behavior Therapy

www.beckinstitute.org

List of International Cognitive Behavioral Therapy Associations

www.cognitivetherapynyc.org/international

National Alliance on Mental Illness

www.nami.org

National Association of Cognitive-Behavioral Therapists

www.nacbt.org

National Institute of Mental Health

www.nimh.nih.gov

www.ingramcontent.com/pod-product-compliance
Lightning Source LLC
Chambersburg PA
CBHW050541280326
41933CB00011B/1679